Images
of
New Jersey

First Printing October, 1991
Robert D. Shangle, Publisher

Library of Congress Cataloging-in-Publication Data
Images of New Jersey
p. cm. ISBN 1-55988-301-4 (soft bound): $6.95
1. New Jersey — Description and travel — 1981 — Views. I. LTA Publishing Company.
F135.I43 1991 917.4904'43 — dc20 91-22801 CIP

Copyright © 1991 by LTA Publishing Company
Production, Concept and Distribution by LTA Publishing Company, Portland, Oregon.
Printed in Thailand. This book produced as the major component of the "World Peace and
Understanding" program of Beauty of America Printing Company, Portland, Oregon.

Introduction

"What a beautiful area!" "I want to remember this forever!" "It's absolutely awesome!" "The Creator simply out-did Himself!"

All of these statements are descriptive of the thoughts expressed when viewing this great state of New Jersey that we live in, work in, and play in. And why not. This is a Grand Place.

Images linger in our mind's eye, bringing back those memories of excitement, happiness, family, loved ones, places we've visited, or always dreamed of visiting. One can remember, either because "I've been there," or visited vicariously. We want to hold onto those experiences of "places I've been, things I've done, places I want to see."

The images in this book have been gathered together to assist with those memories and you can give it life. Combining these pictures with your memories make them fill with energy, telling your story that is full of excitement and thrills.

A tribute to New Jersey!

Atlantic City

Ironmasters Mansion, Batsto

Old Red Mill at Clinton

Atlantic City

The Wading River

Barnegat Lighthouse

Atlantic City

In Allaire Village State Park

Historic Van Sykles Corner at Clinton

Wilk Farm, Morristown Battlefield National Historic Park

Ocean City

Historic Grange Building, Cold Spring

Musconetcong River near Waterloo Village

Marina at Trump Castle, Atlantic City

Cape May

Cape May

In The New Jersey Pine Barrens

Hereford Inlet Lighthouse

The Ford Mansion, Morristown Battlefield National Historic Site (George Washington's Headquarters)

On The Boardwalk, Atlantic City

Asbury Park

Sandy Hook Lighthouse

The New Jersey Pine Barrens

North of Stone Harbor

Atlantic City

Atlantic City

Soldiers' Huts, Morristown Battlefield National Historic Site

The Salem Oak, Over 500 Years Old, Salem

Sailing Off Highland

Near Salem

Barnegat Lighthouse Area

Gateway National Recreation Area

At Cold Spring on Cape May

At Batsto Village State Park

Liberty State Park, Jersey City

Atlantic City

Batsto Lake

Victorian Architecture, Cape May

Gateway National Recreation Area

Highland

Historic Waterloo Village

Absecon Lighthouse, Atlantic City

Allaire Village State Park

Spruce Run State Park

In the New Jersey Pine Barrens

St. Peter by the Sea Church, Cape May

Lewes Ferry, Cape May

Lumpond State Park